August 2010

Dearest Other Daughter~

What a joy to s
with you! May
gain understanding.
read these pages.
I love you very very m
Love & God's Blessings
Other Mom

Living
in the
Power
of the
Holy
Spirit

Living
in the
Power
of the
Holy
Spirit

CHARLES F. STANLEY

Published by
THOMAS NELSON
Since 1798

www.thomasnelson.com

Published in Nashville, Tennessee, by Thomas Nelson, Inc.

All Scripture references in this manuscript are from the NEW KING JAMES VERSION of the Bible. Copyright 1979, 1980, 1982, Thomas Nelson, Inc. Publishers.

Library of Congress Cataloging-in-Publication Data

Stanley, Charles F.
    Living in the power of the Holy Spirit / Charles F. Stanley.
        p. cm.
    ISBN-10: 0-7852-6512-0 (hardcover)
    ISBN-13: 978-0-7852-6512-2 (hardcover)
    1. Holy Spirit. 2. Christian life—Baptist authors. I. Title.
    BT121.3.S73 2005
    231'.3—dc22

                                                            2004030537

Printed in the United States of America

09 10 11 12 13 QW 17 16 15 14 13

CONTENTS

Our Ongoing Success *as* Believers

Once you and I have trusted the Lord Jesus Christ as our Savior, we have the opportunity to learn spiritual principles by which we are to live the Christian life. Many believers, however, find that after a period of time in applying those principles, they incorrectly begin to feel self-confident in their "success" at living the Christian life. And the next thing you know, they've experienced a spiritual setback or moral fall of some kind.

Why is it that we often seem to start strongly in our Christian walk, and then later discover that we are facing failure in our faith?

One of the primary reasons is that we drift away from the very principles that we learned at the beginning of our relationship with Christ. Another key reason is that we become so familiar with the Word of God and the messages that we hear preached that we no longer take the truth of God's Word to heart as diligently and as eagerly as we once did.

Yet a third reason—and perhaps the most prevalent—is that we stop relying on the Holy Spirit to lead us, to guide us, to give us the spiritual power we need to withstand temptation, and to give us the spiritual wisdom we need to recognize and to avoid error.

We never spiritually outgrow our dependency upon the Holy Spirit. The exact opposite is true. The more mature we are in our faith and the more intimate our relationship with our heavenly Father, the more dependent we must be on the Holy Spirit.

It is the Holy Spirit who guides us into the right path for us to walk and convicts us of our sin if we stray from that path.

It is the Holy Spirit who reminds us of the truth of God's Word and teaches us how to apply God's Word to our daily lives.

It is the Holy Spirit who works in us to conform us to the image of Christ Jesus, and who works through us to minister the presence and power of Christ to others.

The ongoing lesson all Christians must learn is how to experience and live *daily* in the power of the Holy Spirit! No matter where you are in your journey with the Lord, this is the key to your being a truly successful Christian.

The Promise of God the Father

Who is the Holy Spirit in the life of the believer today?

The foremost lesson I believe every Christian must learn about the Holy Spirit is this: the Holy Spirit is the Promise of our heavenly Father to *each one of us*.

In Luke 24, we find a very specific command given by Jesus right before He ascends to heaven:

[Jesus] said to them, "These are the words which I spoke to you while I was still with you, that all things must be fulfilled which were written in the Law of Moses and the Prophets and the Psalms concerning Me . . . Thus it is written, and thus it was necessary for the Christ to suffer and to rise from the dead the third day, and that repentance and remission of sins should be preached in His name to all nations, beginning at Jerusalem. And you are witnesses of these things. Behold, I send the Promise of My Father upon you; but tarry in the city of Jerusalem until you are endued [or clothed] with power from on high."

And He led them out as far as Bethany, and He lifted up His hands and blessed them. Now it came to pass, while He blessed them, that He was parted from them and carried up into heaven. And they worshiped Him, and returned to Jerusalem with great joy, and were continually in the temple praising and blessing God. (Luke 24:44–53)

In this very short and simple message to His followers, Jesus gave them the key to living a victorious life as He demonstrated on the earth: "Behold, I send the Promise of My Father upon you."

That Promise—as we know from John 14–15, Acts 1, and other passages in the New Testament—was and is the Holy Spirit. The Promise of Jesus to His disciples at the time of His ascension is the same Promise given by Jesus to those of us who are followers or disciples of Jesus today.

Jesus has made available to every believer the work and power of the Holy Spirit. Every believer receives that promise, regardless of denomination, cultural background, race, color, or age.

Many people seem to think that the Holy Spirit has only been poured out on those who are preachers, teachers, missionaries, or some other type of full-time Christian worker. Not so! The anointing power of the Holy Spirit is for every believer—the Holy Spirit has been given to businessmen, mothers, students, plumbers, secretaries, and to people in all walks of life.

GOD'S DIVINE PRESENCE AND SOVEREIGN POWER

What does the Bible mean by the power of the Holy Spirit—the "power from on high"?

The power of the Holy Spirit is the divine authority and energy that God releases into the life of every one of His children in order that we might live a godly and fruitful life. The Word tells us that we become "clothed from on high" by this power—it envelops us, not only covering us and protecting us from the influence of the devil, but also enabling us to demonstrate the likeness of Christ.

The Holy Spirit covers us in such a way that we bear both the fruit of His character and the demonstration of His presence wherever we go. Clothing identifies people as having authority, prestige, or influence— such as the uniform of a policeman, the cloak of a king, or the robes of a judge. Similarly the spiritual "garment" bestowed by the Holy Spirit identifies us as Christ's own brothers or sisters alive and at work in this world.

WE CANNOT MANIPULATE THE HOLY SPIRIT

What does the Bible mean when Jesus said His disciples would be "endued with power"? It means that the Holy Spirit initiates and governs His relationship with us from start to finish.

The Holy Spirit cannot be manipulated. You cannot make the Holy Spirit do anything. You cannot fill yourself with the Holy Spirit, no matter what formula or method or series of works you perform. You cannot govern the Holy Spirit. Neither can you eliminate the Holy Spirit from your life.

God imparts His Spirit to those who believe in Jesus Christ as their Savior. The work that the Holy Spirit does in our lives is *His* work, done at *His* initiative, motivated by *His* love and divine purpose for our lives. The Holy Spirit manifests Himself as *He* desires in our lives.

It is the Holy Spirit who does the work—

- energizing the body, both individually and corporately as the church,

- enlightening and renewing the mind to understand truth and apply it in our daily lives,

- inflaming our hearts with a passion of devotion to Almighty God,

- and generating in us a tremendous desire to preach repentance and remission of sins to all nations.

THE PROMISE OF THE FATHER

What does the Bible mean when it refers to the Holy Spirit as the "Promise" of God?

A promise is something that is always and forever. Jesus was indicating that the Holy Spirit will *always* be with us as our Comforter, our Helper, our Source of divine power, and the One who leads us into all truth.

Jesus said to His disciples that when they receive this Promise of the Father, "You will know that I am in My Father, and you in Me, and I in you." We are endued or "clothed" by the Holy Spirit; we have a knowing that we are in Christ and He dwells in us in the form of the Holy Spirit *always*. The Holy Spirit is God's assurance that our salvation is secure—it is *promised* to us for all eternity.

What a great mystery and wonder this is! We are in

Christ. He dwells in us by His Spirit. What a tremendous promise! And most amazingly, this promise is the gift to every believer.

In Acts 2, we find a powerful sermon preached by the apostle Peter after the Holy Spirit had been poured out upon a group of faithful disciples. These disciples had been praying and praising God continually from the time of Jesus' ascension for ten days until the feast of Pentecost. At the close of Peter's sermon, the people were so convicted of their sin that they cried out to Peter and the other apostles:

> "Men and brethren, what shall we do?"
>
> [Peter replied] to them, "Repent, and let every one of you be baptized in the name of Jesus Christ for the remission of sins; and you shall receive the gift of the Holy Spirit. For the promise is to you and to your children, and to all who are afar off, as many as the Lord our God will call." (Acts 2:37–39)

The Holy Spirit is God's promise to *you*. You *shall* receive the Holy Spirit when you admit to your sin and turn from it and receive Jesus Christ as your Savior. Believe that He alone has provided the full and final sacrifice for your sin—and determine that you will turn from your past life and follow Jesus Christ as your Lord every day of your future.

2

Who Is the Holy Spirit?

The Bible tells us very clearly who the Holy Spirit is—He is a person of the Trinity. He is *God the Holy Spirit.*

In Genesis 1, we read:

In the beginning God created the heavens and the earth. The earth was without form, and void; and darkness was on the face of the deep. And the Spirit of God was hovering over the face of the waters . . .

Then God said, "Let Us make man in Our image, according to Our likeness; let them have dominion over the fish of the sea, over the birds of the air, and over the cattle, over all the earth and over every creeping thing that creeps on the earth." (Gen. 1:1–2, 26)

It is the Holy Spirit who was brooding over the waters at the outset of Creation. When the Bible refers to *Our* image and likeness, it is referring to the fullness of God—God the Father, God the Son, and God the Holy Spirit.

In the gospel of John, we find Jesus encouraging His disciples just prior to His arrest in the Garden of Gethsemane. He says to them:

> I will pray the Father, and He will give you another Helper, that He may abide with you forever—the Spirit of truth, whom the world cannot receive, because it neither sees Him nor knows Him; but you know Him, for He dwells with you and will be in you. I will not leave you orphans; I will come to you. (John 14:16–18)

Jesus refers to the Holy Spirit as *He*—a person of the Trinity—not an "it." He is One with the Father, just as Jesus and the Father are One. He is One with Jesus. He is *God* the Holy Spirit.

The apostle Paul affirmed the personhood of the

Holy Spirit in writing to the Romans: "Likewise the Spirit also helps in our weaknesses. For we do not know what we should pray for as we ought, but the Spirit Himself makes intercession for us with groanings which cannot be uttered" (Rom. 8:26).

THE HOLY SPIRIT IS NOT A GHOST

The King James Version of the Bible refers to the Holy Spirit in a number of places as the Holy Ghost. While that may have been an accurate translation at the time of King James, the word *ghost* has come to mean other things. The Holy Spirit is not an apparition, floating about here and there and manifesting Himself in a mysterious, now-you-see-Him, now-you-don't manner. The proper translation of this term for today is the Holy *Spirit*. The Holy Spirit is the very essence of God.

The true you is not your body—if the Lord does not return in your lifetime, your body will die. At death, the difference between a person's body and a person's spirit becomes very clear. So, too, with God the Holy

Spirit. The Holy Spirit is the living *personhood of God*, not manifested in a fleshly body—that manifestation was Jesus—but manifested nonetheless as the full personality and identity of God *resident in us as believers*.

The Spirit of the living God is not a "force." He is *Somebody*.

If anyone ever asks you, "Who is the Holy Spirit?" I hope you will be quick to respond, "He is a person of the Trinity—He is God the Holy Spirit." And immediately, I hope you add, "He is God's Promise to me, God's gift to me as a believer. The Holy Spirit is resident in me."

How Do We Receive the Holy Spirit?

There are many Christians who seem to believe that the Holy Spirit is imparted to them through some type of action taken by an ordained minister—it may be a prayer, the laying on of hands, the pronouncement of a blessing, or some other deed. The Bible, however, tells us very clearly that God the Father gives the Holy Spirit.

One of the reasons people tend to think of the Holy Spirit as "it" instead of "He" is because they are thinking of the Holy Spirit as a force or type of power, rather than the Spirit of God. I hear people all the time say about the indwelling presence of the Holy Spirit, "When did you get it?" The emphasis is usually placed upon a particular manifestation of the Holy Spirit—a "sign" of His indwelling presence. That sign might be speaking in other tongues, falling under the power of the Holy Spirit, shaking or quaking, displaying an outpouring of laughter, or any other sign that has come to be associated with the Holy Spirit's presence in the mind of a particular believer.

The problem with associating the Holy Spirit with a particular *sign* is that we limit the Holy Spirit to that singular expression. Those who have this perspective tend to think that the Holy Spirit is only present when that particular sign is manifested. The truth is, the Holy Spirit is not limited to any one particular sign or manifestation—He is the omnipotent, omnipresent, omniscient, all-loving God. He is so far greater than any particular manifestation! We do the Holy Spirit a grave injustice any time we identify Him by His signs rather than by His nature as a person of the Trinity.

The real question to ask about the Holy Spirit is: "When did you receive Him?"

The answer? You received Him the moment you received Jesus as your Savior. That's what God says in His Word: "Repent, and let every one of you be baptized in the name of Jesus Christ for the remission of sins; and you shall receive the gift of the Holy Spirit" (Acts 2:38).

It is the Holy Spirit who baptizes us into Christ—He is the One who completely covers us with the redemptive shed blood and living presence of Christ Jesus. It is the Holy Spirit who gives us our new identity in Christ so that we truly are born again spiritually. It is Jesus, now sitting at the right hand of the Father, who sends to us His own Spirit to dwell in us. Jesus is no longer with us on earth—but His same Spirit dwells in us (see John 14:17).

In receiving what Jesus did on your behalf and believing with your will and faith that He is the One who purchased the remission of sins for you through

His death on the Cross, you are *receiving* Christ Jesus into your life. You cannot receive just a part of God. In receiving God the Son, you *are receiving the fullness of God into your life.* That *person* of God, who resides within you—dwells in you, abides in you, fills you—is God the Holy Spirit. It is in the form of the Holy Spirit that God comes to live in us.

Oh, what a tremendous gift God has given us! He has given us *Himself.* He has given us the *fullness* of His own nature that we truly might be created anew spiritually in His likeness, in His image.

3

Why Does God Send *the* Holy Spirit *to* Us?

Why does God send the Holy Spirit to dwell within you and me as believers in Christ Jesus? There are two main reasons:

- First, the Holy Spirit enables and empowers us to "be" witnesses of Christ Jesus to a lost and dying world.

- Second, the Holy Spirit enables and empowers us to "do" the ministry of Christ Jesus in our service to other believers.

ENABLING POWER TO "BE" WITNESSES FOR CHRIST JESUS

I frequently encounter Christians who believe that only certain people are "called" by God to accomplish specific tasks on this earth. The categories of people they believe are called include preachers, apostles, evangelists, teachers, pastors, missionaries, and so forth. The Bible tells us, however, that all believers are called *according to God's purpose* (see Romans 8:28). Does God purpose that the gospel of Jesus be on the lips of all believers? Absolutely. Does God purpose that each one of us should be quick to tell a lost sinner how to accept Jesus as his Savior? Absolutely. Does God purpose that each one of us show by our lives that we have been saved? Absolutely. We are *all* called to be witnesses. Jesus said:

> You shall receive power when the Holy Spirit has come upon you; and *you shall be witnesses to Me in Jerusalem, and in all Judea and Samaria, and to the end of the earth.* (Acts 1:8; emphasis added)

Not every person is called to be a preacher, pastor, missionary, evangelist, or Bible teacher. Some are called to be businessmen, mothers, and carpenters—name any honorable profession or vocation you choose. God *calls* people to fill every niche of society with His presence and power. It is in that manner that we truly become "leaven in the loaf" of the world—evenly distributed into every aspect of society so that we might influence the *whole* of this world for Christ Jesus.

Not every person is going to turn on a Christian radio or television program, or walk into a church to hear the gospel preached. That's why God places His witnesses into every sector of society and in every type of circumstance and situation. *Every* believer is called by God to be a witness for Jesus Christ in the world in which God has placed him or her. *Every* believer can speak the name of Jesus in the marketplace, the hospital, the courtroom, the classroom, the family kitchen, the construction site, the factory floor, the sports arena, or any other place the believer may be. God's desire is that *all* may hear, experience, and receive His gospel. He speaks through us and through our actions to people we don't even know we are influencing for Christ.

Can any of us be an effective witness to the saving

grace of Jesus Christ through reliance on our own strength, ability, and power? No. We all are subject to temptations, to peer pressure, to ungodly influences. Our salvation does not keep us from the pressures and temptations of the world. Our salvation does not automatically ensure that we will never fail, err, or make a bad decision.

The Holy Spirit dwelling in us *enables* us, however, to live a godly life and to express—through our words and deeds—the good news of Jesus Christ with simplicity, clarity, and effectiveness. The Holy Spirit gives us:

- *Wisdom.* The Holy Spirit is also called the Spirit of Truth—the One who guides us into making God's choices and decisions. He is the One who leads us to the discovery of God's solutions and the formation of God's plans. Every person needs God's wisdom in how to raise children or to influence the children of others for Christ, manage his finances, run his business or career, plan for his retirement, have godly relationships, and function in his God-given spiritual gifts. We are all in desperate need of wisdom to make it safely, productively, and joyfully through any given day!

- *Enduring strength.* The Holy Spirit is the source of all spiritual power. The Holy Spirit not only gives us the power from time to time to function in miraculous ways for the benefit of others, but He gives us the enduring, persevering, lasting power to withstand any persecution until God defeats our enemies. I have met many people who tell me that they experience bursts of spiritual growth from time to time, and they also experience spiritual "deserts" or spiritually dry times. Let me encourage you—the Holy Spirit resides within you, the believer, to give you the staying power you need to grow steadily and remain steadfast in your faith regardless of circumstances around you or feelings that ebb and flow like the tide.

- *Courage.* The Holy Spirit is our Comforter, the One who walks alongside us to encourage us and to infuse us with His abiding presence. His presence gives us the courage to take on evil and *win!* None of us are strong enough to take on the devil alone. We each need the Holy Spirit at work in us, through us, and on our behalf if we are to defeat evil and emerge victorious in our lives.

- *An ability to withstand temptation.* The Holy Spirit does not immunize us against temptation—rather, He enables us to withstand temptation. He imparts to us the ability to turn away from all things that are contrary to God's plan and purpose for our lives. In Luke 4 we read that Jesus, our prime example of this, was filled with the Holy Spirit and then immediately was led by the Holy Spirit into the wilderness. There Jesus was tempted for forty days by the devil. At the end of those forty days, Jesus returned to Galilee "in the power of the Holy Spirit." It was the Spirit who enabled Jesus to say no to the basic

temptations given to all people: material substance, fame, and power (see Luke 4:1–2). Every
one of us needs God's *power* to infuse our *will* so
that we truly have *willpower*.

It is as we express God's wisdom, strength, courage,
and fortitude to say no to temptation that we are witnesses to Christ Jesus by our actions, as well as by our
words. It is God's Holy Spirit enabling us to speak and to
act wisely, consistently over time, boldly on behalf of
what is right, and in a godly manner. Our exercising good
judgment reveals the Holy Spirit within us, and that says
to the world, "There's something different about that
man . . . There's something different about that woman."
The Holy Spirit enables us to live truly changed, dynamic,
and vibrant lives so that others will *want* to know the
source of our joy and peace and confidence. The Holy
Spirit working in us and through us sets the stage for us
to proclaim the truth that Jesus is the only begotten Son
of God, who died for our sins that we might be born
again spiritually and begin to receive the gift of eternal
life.

ENABLING POWER TO "DO" THE
MINISTRY OF CHRIST JESUS

Apart from our daily walk and witness, we are empowered by the Holy Spirit to engage powerfully and enthusiastically in the specific ministry that God has given to us.

It was after Jesus returned from the temptation in the wilderness that He began His active teaching and healing ministry. The Bible tells us that news about Him spread throughout the region and, as He taught in the synagogues, He was "glorified by all" (Luke 4:15). When Jesus came to Nazareth, He opened the scroll in the synagogue on the Sabbath day and read these words from Isaiah:

The Spirit of the LORD is upon Me,
Because He has anointed Me
To preach the gospel to the poor;
He has sent Me to heal the brokenhearted,
To proclaim liberty to the captives
And recovery of sight to the blind,

To set at liberty those who are oppressed;

To proclaim the acceptable year of the LORD.

(Luke 4:18–19; Isaiah 61:1–2)

Jesus made it very clear that the Spirit was upon Him to anoint Him for the specific ministry that lay ahead for Him.

Prior to Jesus' wilderness experience, He was living and working in Nazareth. Then John the Baptist baptized Him and the Spirit of God came upon Him. He was led by the Spirit into the wilderness and strengthened by the Spirit as He defeated the devil's temptations. He then returned to Galilee "in the power of the Spirit," and the fullness of His ministry was released.

Think also of Paul—known at that time as Saul—who had a divine encounter with the Lord while he was on his way to Damascus to persecute the Christians there (see Acts 8–9). Saul yielded himself to Christ's message and was led blind and trembling into Damascus, where he remained for three days, neither eating nor drinking.

Then a disciple in Damascus named Ananias was instructed by the Lord to go to Saul. Ananias laid hands on him and said, "Brother Saul, the Lord Jesus, who appeared to you on the road as you came, has sent me that you may receive your sight and be filled with the Holy Spirit." And immediately, Saul received his sight, was baptized, received food and was strengthened, and "preached the Christ in the synagogues, that Christ is the Son of God." The people were amazed—Saul went from being a zealot intent on the destruction of all Christians to being an evangelist boldly proclaiming Jesus as Christ! The Pharisees and Sadducees who heard him were baffled and angry—so angry, in fact, they sought to assassinate him.

What made the difference in Paul's life? The indwelling power of the Holy Spirit that he experienced as a result of believing in Jesus Christ.

What is true for Jesus and Paul is also true for you. One of the primary reasons the Holy Spirit indwells your life is so you can boldly and effectively do the ministry that God has called and prepared you to perform. God would not indwell you if He did not intend for you to do something in your life for His sake. He intends to work through you to accomplish His purposes on this earth. God gives you His supernatural power in order to do supernatural work. He imparts to you His divine energy and His divine authority so that you may participate fully and successfully in His divine plan.

"But," you may be saying, "I'm not called to be a pastor or an evangelist." Perhaps not, but you *are* called to some form of ministry. God imparts one or more *spiritual gifts* to those who believe in Christ Jesus—we sometimes refer to these as "ministry gifts." Romans 12 lists these gifts:

Having then gifts differing according to the grace that is given to us, let us use them: if prophecy, let us prophesy in proportion to our faith; or ministry, let us use it in our ministering; he who teaches, in teaching; he who exhorts, in exhortation; he who gives, with liberality; he who leads, with diligence; he who shows mercy, with cheerfulness. (Rom. 12:6–8)

These gifts are resident in us. They do not leave us, although they may lie dormant in us. As we develop and use our gifts we grow in our ability to help others. As we help others by using our God-imparted gifts we fulfill our purpose on earth. As we fulfill God's purpose for us, we experience a twofold reward: we are effective witnesses for the gospel, which bears great *heavenly* reward, and we experience a great deal of personal satisfaction and joy, which is our *earthly* reward.

OUR RESPONSE TO THE HOLY SPIRIT'S POWER IN US

Once you have believed in Jesus Christ and received the Holy Spirit, you can never again say, "I can't do that" when God calls you to do something. Why? Because God has given you the Holy Spirit to indwell you and to enable you. The Holy Spirit in you says "You *can*" in every situation where you might otherwise say "I can't."

There is only one option left to the believer when God calls him to say or to do something, and that is obedience. There is only one right response when God calls, and that is to say, "Yes, here am I."

You may be thinking, *But I'm not adequate.* Friend, none of us is adequate in our own strength and wisdom. But in Christ, *all* of us are made adequate by the Holy Spirit! Any time you are feeling inadequate, there are three things you should do:

- *First, recognize your need of the Lord.* Admit to the Lord that you need His help, His wisdom, His strength, His power, His resources, His protection, and His provision.

- *Second, rely upon Him.* Trust God to be faithful to His word that He will never leave you nor forsake you. He will provide fully for all things that He calls you to do. He will do and be in us everything we need for Him to do and to be.

- *Third, take a step in faith to act upon what He has called you to do.* Nobody can steer or guide a parked car into right position—it is only as the car is put in gear, the accelerator is applied, and the car begins to move that the car can be maneuvered. In a like manner, God guides and directs us *as we move toward the goal He sets before us.*

None of us can do the ministry that God gives us on our own. That is part of God's plan. We *must* have His Holy Spirit at work in us.

Why did God send the Holy Spirit?

- *To enable us to be His witnesses.* The Holy Spirit gives us the wisdom, strength, comfort, and power to act and to speak in a way that reflects Christ Jesus.

- *To enable us to do His supernatural work.* The Holy Spirit in us gives us the strength, power, and wisdom to become active in our God-ordained service to others.

The Holy Spirit enables us to accomplish what we were designed for from our birth and designated for since our spiritual rebirth.

4

The Release *of* Your Full Potential

Every one of us has been given *natural* and *supernatural* gifts. Our natural gifts are imparted to us at our physical birth; our spiritual gifts are imparted to us at our spiritual rebirth. These gifts may lie unused and dormant within us for long periods of time or even for all of our life. Both types of gifts require that we work to develop them.

Now there are some folk out there who seem to do pretty well in their lives by using only their natural abilities. At least, we *think* they are doing well.

In truth, no person using his natural abilities alone can arrive at the *fullness* of what God has planned for him. Why? Because God created us with the capacity for *spiritual* abilities. Unless we are using both our natural *and* spiritual abilities to their maximum potential, we are falling short of complete fulfillment of our life's purpose.

THE POTENTIAL THAT LIES WITHIN YOU

God gives every person a potential, and He alone knows the extent of that potential. None of us knows *all* that we can become or do with the built-in natural and spiritual abilities God imparts to us. The question we each must ask ourselves is not *How much potential do I have?* but rather *Am I living in the fullness of my potential?* The answer is always no. Each one of us can still become more and do more than we are at the present. We never reach the limits of what we can do *in Christ Jesus*. There is always more for the believer.

How can this be? Because an unlimited God has chosen to indwell us. When we reach the end of who we are in the flesh, we are only at the beginning of what the Holy Spirit can do with our spirits!

God is omnipotent. He has all power. When we run

out of our natural strength and power, we are only at the beginning of His power.

God is omniscient. He has all wisdom. When we run out of our natural mental ability to understand and create, we have barely tapped God's wisdom and creativity.

God is omnipresent. He is both eternal and ever-present in every moment. When we run out of time in any given day or at the end of our lives, we have yet to experience a nanosecond of God's eternity. When we become frustrated at our inability to be in two places at once or to give our full time to any given pursuit, we are only at the beginning of God's ability to be present with us always.

God is all-loving. He never fails to extend His mercy and lovingkindness to all who open their hearts to receive Him. As much as we may try to show forgiveness, mercy, and kindness to others, we are only at the beginning of God's infinite love.

I know with certainty that those who truly are filled with God's Spirit *want* to pursue their potential to expand their capacity to help others and improve the quality of their impact on others. The genuinely Spirit-filled person will not be calloused toward others, careless or slothful in work, indifferent in responsibility, or satisfied with mediocrity. Why do I make this claim? Because God, our Creator, does not display any of those qualities in either His creation of us or His provision for us.

God is *always available* to those who call on Him.

God *never wastes anything*—He uses everything given to Him and multiplies it for His purposes and our blessing.

God is *always on time*—He is never too early or too late.

God *never gives partial attention or partial concern to a matter*—He gives His all, His utmost, His highest, His best, His full attention, and His full compassion.

God is *always creating good*—He does all things with excellence and for maximum benefit.

If every Christian in America lived in the fullness of the Holy Spirit, I can only begin to imagine what might happen in our economy. I believe it would explode internationally in such a way that there'd be no human explanation for it.

If every believer in America went to work each morning full of the Holy Spirit and desiring to do their best, the quality of work and the productivity of the workplace would improve. If every believer gave their all with a right motivation and absolute dependence upon God, attitudes would be better and morale would begin to rise. Those with joy in their hearts would come up with more ideas and innovations than ever thought possible!

If every believer in America arose each day with an attitude of expressing the love of God to family members and friends, as well as to every stranger encountered during the day, we would no longer see the manifestations of hatred, anger, and distrust, such as road rage, violent behavior, crime, and all forms of abuse.

God the Holy Spirit energizes our bodies, enlightens our minds, and inflames the passions of our hearts so we might move forward into and expand our potential. The Holy Spirit motivates us to reach for our potential

and enables us to make progress toward the full manifestation of our potential.

THREE GREAT AREAS OF POTENTIAL

There are three areas of potential that are especially
important to God. God desires that you pursue:

- *The full potential of your love.* None of us loves
  others as we know we should or even as we want
  to love. We all say things we know later we
  shouldn't have said. We all do things we regret in
  hindsight. We all willfully choose to do things
  that are pleasing to our own selves at the expense
  of others. We all make mistakes when it comes to
  giving time and attention to those nearest and
  dearest to us.

It is the Holy Spirit who continually prompts us to
find new ways of reaching out to others with genuine
compassion and godly love. The Holy Spirit constantly
points out to us areas in which He desires for us to

move beyond our own self-centered wants and to help others in material and practical ways. The Holy Spirit compels us to love as Christ Jesus loved us with a heart that refuses to judge or condemn, a heart willing to sacrifice so that others might be saved. The Holy Spirit prompts us to encourage and exhort and embrace others so that, as the body of Christ, we might grow toward maturity.

Do you have a desire today to love God and to love others more, with a purer heart and mind, and with greater compassion and expressions of generosity? Ask the Holy Spirit to help you reach your full potential to *love*.

- *The full potential of your obedience.* In our own strength, none of us obeys God perfectly. Even when we desire to do God's will, we all make errors in timing, judgment, choices, and decisions. We all fall short in our efforts and behavior. The Holy Spirit helps us to obey God *quickly* and *fully*. The Holy Spirit gives us the *desire* to obey God, even when His commands to us are not what we desire in the flesh. The Holy Spirit leads us into "right paths" so that we obey God, not only when it comes to the big issues of life, but in our moment-by-moment daily decisions as well.

Do you have a desire today to obey God more completely and quickly, with fewer arguments, justifications, or excuses? Ask the Holy Spirit to help you reach your full potential to obey.

- *The full potential of your devotion.* None of us is as devoted or steadfast in our walk with the Lord as we would like to be. We all are quick to want to do our own thing—from sleeping in on a Sunday morning to willfully choosing to participate in an activity that we know is contrary to God's best. We all know that we should praise and thank God more, pray more, read the Bible more, and be more involved in the life of the church we attend. The Holy Spirit gives us the desire to spend more time with God. The Holy Spirit gives us a new song of praise to the Lord. The Holy Spirit prays at the deepest part of our being so that our prayers are in the center of God's will for us and gives us insight into the meaning and application of the Scriptures to our own life. The Holy Spirit infuses our churches so they overflow with joy and the healing and forgiving power of God.

Do you have a desire today to follow God more closely and steadfastly and to experience greater intimacy with God? Do you have a desire today to experience more of God's power flowing in you and through you to others? Ask the Holy Spirit to help you reach your full potential of faith and devotion.

FOUR GREAT QUESTIONS TO ASK GOD EVERY DAY

From time to time, I meet people who are having a hard time and who sometimes admit they are discouraged and depressed. As I ask them for details about their lives, I often discover that they are acting totally on their own strength and energy. They are trusting in their experience, their education, their acquired skills, and their natural know-how. In some cases, they are trusting in others to provide for them. Their discouragement is rooted in the fact that they are failing in some way or others are failing them. They are disappointed in themselves or in others.

Friend, any time you try to define and reach your own potential using human resources alone . . . you are going to fail. And the more you fail or feel that others have failed you, the more you are going to be subject to disappointment, discouragement, and depression.

The real key to reaching your potential lies in trusting God to help you become your best. We do this by actively and verbally placing our trust in the Lord, saying, "I need You, Holy Spirit, to help me become and do all that God has created me to be and do. I need You, Holy Spirit, to work in me in such a way that I will want to accomplish and be able to accomplish all that You have purposed for me to do in my life."

There are four great questions we are wise to ask God daily:

1. *What do You want me to do?* God desires to reveal to you the next step you can take into your own potential. Ask the Holy Spirit to reveal to you specifically what He desires for you to do in any given day. Is there someone He desires for you to contact? Is there someone He is planning to bring across your path? Is there a meeting you should attend or an appointment you should make? Is there a decision you should make?

Be open to the promptings of the Holy Spirit deep within your heart. Trust Him to give you precise guidance and direction.

2. *How do You want me to act?* For everything that God desires to accomplish on this earth, He has a *method* He plans to use. For every purpose, there is an accompanying plan. Ask the Holy Spirit to show you *how* you are to accomplish the goals He sets before you. What methodology or protocol should you use?

3. *When do You want me to act?* We often fail because we get ahead of God, or we lag behind. For every thing that God desires to accomplish on this earth, He has a precise timetable. Ask the Holy Spirit

to show you His schedule and His expansion plan. When you act can be as important as how you act and what you do.

4. *How can I best represent You today?* The Holy Spirit desires to influence others not only through what you do and say, but also by your very presence in any group of people. Ask the Holy Spirit to give you the joy, peace, and forgiving spirit that bear witness to Christ Jesus. Ask the Holy Spirit to make and mold you into an even greater likeness of Christ.

Listen closely for God's answers to your questions. Some of those answers are likely to be revealed to you as you read and study your Bible on a consistent, daily basis. Some answers may come as you hear a Bible-based, gospel-infused, Spirit-filled sermon or teaching tape. Some of those answers may come as you listen quietly before the Lord. Some answers may come as you receive godly counsel from believers who are skilled in their fields and humble in their hearts before God.

When you know God's answers . . . and *only* when you know God's answers . . . begin to act. Stay sensitive to the Lord all day. Ask repeatedly, "Is this what You want me to do? Am I doing this in the way that is pleasing to You? Am I on Your schedule? Am I reflecting You in a way that brings glory to Your name?"

TRUST GOD TO REWARD YOU

Many people today promote themselves so that others will reward them with raises, new job titles, and greater benefits. Some promote themselves so that others will vote for them, honor them, give them greater recognition, or increase their fame. The believer should rest in confidence that the Holy Spirit is the One who brings our works to the Father so that He might reward us in His timing, according to His methods, and in the way that is just right for us.

Don't be concerned about whether or not others see your good works. When God sees your good works and the right motives of your heart, *He* will promote you and reward you in the way that brings you to greater personal fulfillment and greater usefulness in His kingdom.

Do every job you are given to do as if you are doing it exclusively for the Lord. It may be cooking a meal, setting a corporate policy, cleaning a house, enacting a law or making a judgment, responding to the skinned knee of a child, answering a phone call, purchasing an object, making a contribution, mowing a yard, building a house, designing a room, or giving a gift. Name any activity you care to name—any part of a job description, no matter how great or small—and I'll show you a job you can do as unto the Lord.

Whatever your hands find to do, work with diligence, perseverance, and to the best of your ability. Work with enthusiasm and expectation that God will see your work and reward you according to His riches.

When you are working with others, work with a spirit of encouragement and patience. Work with respect for the dignity and value of others. Work with integrity.

And then, trust God to use you, to move you, and to place you precisely where He desires. Those who are trustworthy in small things are often made supervisors over great things. This is the message of Jesus' parable of the talents (see Matthew 25:14–30). Those who use their talents with a desire to please the Lord are those who see their talents multiplied and their efforts rewarded! I don't care how old or young you are, what your vocation may be, or your background . . . if you will trust the Holy Spirit to be the One who brings about the rewards for your life, you are going to find yourself greatly blessed.

This is not only true in your professional life, career, or business, but also true in your relationships with other people, especially with your children. Ask the Holy Spirit to do His work in the lives of your children and in your relationship with them. Ask Him to help you work with each child lovingly and patiently to discover and develop that child's natural and spiritual gifts. Ask Him to guide your conversations and behavior with your child so that you might provide maximum help, love, and encouragement to your child. And then, trust God to reward you as a parent and to reward your child as only He can!

Only God sees the beginning from the ending of your life. Only God knows *all* the traits, capacities, abilities, and desires He has placed in you, both naturally and spiritually. Only God knows where you are on His timetable of development. Only God knows the full extent of the circumstances of your life and the full nature of the environment in which you presently live. Only God knows the full agenda He has established for you. And only God knows the richness of the rewards that He has set aside for you both now and in eternity.

The Holy Spirit indwells you to nudge you, prod you, push you, mold you, remake you, and fashion you in the *fullness* of all that God has for you. The Holy Spirit is at work in you to be the developer of your life—bringing all of your talents and abilities to the fullness of their use both naturally and spiritually.

5

A Life
of
Holiness

The Holy Spirit is God's *holy* Spirit. We sometimes lose sight of that word *holy* when we refer to the Spirit or when we discuss the work of the Spirit in our lives. God's purpose for indwelling us with His own Spirit is to make us *holy*. In 1 Peter 1:15–16 we read, "As He who called you is holy, you also be holy in all your conduct, because it is written, 'Be holy, for I am holy.'" We are called to a *holy* life.

Many people shy away from the word *holy* because they don't know what the word means.

Let me tell you three things that a holy life is *not*.

First, a holy life is not a bizarre, separate-yourself-from-humanity life. We as Christians are called to be *in* the world, although we are not to be *of* the world. We are not to separate ourselves physically from other people—rather, we are to build bridges to other people so we might influence them for the gospel and bring them to salvation.

Second, a holy life is not an "as good as I can be" life. Many people have told me through the years, "Well, I'm doing the best I can to do the right things and to be good." They are struggling in their own efforts to win God's favor. Friend, that just doesn't work. None of us can ever do enough good deeds, give large enough contributions, or behave in a good enough manner to earn salvation. The Bible is very clear on this. Ephesians 2:8–9 tells us, "By grace you have been saved through faith, and that not of yourselves; it is the gift of God, not of works, lest anyone should boast."

I have heard a number of people say, "Well, I tried the Christian life and it just doesn't work." My first response is to say, "Well, I've tried it and it *does* work!" The fact is, people who think they've "tried" Christianity have the emphasis on try and try and try and try, rather than on Christ. They are striving in their own strength and their own energy to do what only God can do in them, for them, and through them.

They are trying to save themselves . . . trying to bless themselves . . . trying to change themselves . . . trying to renew themselves. And all of that, my friend, is the work of the Holy Spirit, not the work of man.

The only way to be saved is to accept Jesus Christ as your personal Savior and then rely upon the Holy Spirit to help you repent of your sinful ways and pursue a holy life. The Holy Spirit imparts holiness to you: you cannot become holy through your own natural efforts.

Third, a holy life is not a sinless life. God knows that we are human and that sin is part of the human condition. We all make mistakes, errors of judgment, and bad choices. Any person who says that he does not sin is only fooling himself. In fact, John wrote, "If we say that we have no sin, we deceive ourselves, and the truth is not in us. If we say that we have not sinned, we make Him a liar, and His word is not in us" (1 John 1:8, 10).

Every person was born with a sinful nature (see Romans 3:23). We either let that sinful nature dominate and rule our life, or we have an experience with

Jesus Christ—and it is through Jesus Christ—by which we are saved! Those who confess their sins and ask God's forgiveness *are* forgiven (1 John 1:9). And in place of their old sinful nature, the believer in Christ Jesus receives a new spiritual nature that longs to live according to the commandments of God.

What the Holy Spirit does in our lives is to convict us of sin quickly and decisively. Any and every time we think a thought, speak a word, or behave in a way that is contrary to God's commandments and His desire for us, the Holy Spirit convicts us that we are in error. He speaks to our hearts that our lives are out of alignment with the life that God has authorized for us and granted us the privilege to live. The Holy Spirit gives to us a "want to" desire—not just a "have to" obligation—to live a holy life. We are holy because He is holy and He dwells in us and works through us.

THE HALLMARKS OF A HOLY LIFE

What does it mean, then, to have a holy life? It means that we choose to live according to God's way rather than our own way. It means we choose to be led by the Holy Spirit day by day.

The Bible teaches that we have one of two lifestyles. We either have a lifestyle in the flesh or a lifestyle in the Spirit. We *either* choose to live according to our natural impulses and desires, making decisions and choosing actions solely on the basis of what pleases us personally; *or*, we choose to live according to God's directives, making decisions and choosing actions that He authorizes and compels us to take.

Those who believe in Christ Jesus are given a new spirit, a new nature. They move from living "in the flesh" to living "in the Spirit." Does that mean that we completely lose our natural, fleshly impulses and desires? No—we still live in physical bodies in a natural world and have a physical brain that has been trained to think in certain habitual ways. Life in the Spirit becomes our *desire*, but that life is not automatically acquired. We must learn to walk in that new life, learn to think in a new way that the Bible calls the "renewal of the mind," and develop new ways of responding to life's problems and circumstances.

It would be wonderful, of course, if God would take away all of our natural desires when we accept Jesus Christ as our Savior. But He doesn't. We still have a capacity to sin against God any time we choose to. We still possess our free will and we still have the capacity to be tempted. None of us ever outgrows our natural, physical, fleshly carnality.

We've all heard people say, "Well, what I do is just natural." Or, "it's just not natural to live a life according to God's commandments." They are correct! Most people live according to what they regard as natural. It's natural for a lost man or woman to want to live in a way that is physically gratifying and sexually immoral. It's not the natural impulse automatically to choose to live a holy life.

The apostle Paul wrote to the Ephesians:

And you He made alive, who were dead in trespasses and sins, in which you once walked according to the course of this world, according to the prince of the power of the air, the spirit who now works in the sons of disobedience, among whom also we all once conducted ourselves in the lusts of our flesh, fulfilling the desires of the flesh and of the mind, and were by nature children of wrath, just as the others. (Eph. 2:1–3)

God has created a place in each of our lives that only Jesus can fill, and until He is invited to fill that place, man searches for something that will satisfy his need for love, acceptance, and satisfaction. Mankind turns to what he can *sense* and know in the physical and natural realm, and his restless search is endless until he invites Jesus to fill his life.

When the Holy Spirit indwells our lives, He changes our desires, our needs, and our innermost goals—not necessarily eliminating our desires, needs, or goals but *changing them*. Even so, the saying is true, "old habits die hard." Most of us have developed a habit of thinking certain ways, acting in certain ways, and responding to certain situations in certain ways. It takes time and intentional effort to change those patterns of thinking and behaving.

Can we make this change in our response pattern to

life? No. We may choose to change many things in our life—the power of the human will is strong—but we cannot change our basic response pattern. Our response pattern to life is deeply rooted in our personality and our character. Only the Holy Spirit can change our perspective on life, our response to life, and our evaluation of life.

One of the most awesome moments in my life occurred the night I realized for the first time that I could not live the Christian life that God desired for me in the manner that I was living. I repeatedly tried begging, praying, pleading, fasting, and trying again and again and again to change certain things in the way I thought, felt, and acted. The more I *tried* to be godly, the more I felt like an absolute failure. Then I read the first chapter in Hudson Taylor's classic little book, *They Found the Secret.* I recognized what Jesus meant when He said, "I am the vine, you are the branches. He who abides in Me, and I in him, bears much fruit; for without Me you can do nothing" (John 15:5).

No branch of any vine is able to bear fruit if it is

separated from the vine. The branch lives off the vine. It's the sap running from the vine down into the branches that produces the fruit. The sap does not change nature as it runs from the vine into the branch—it's the same life-giving force. Neither does the sap flow at the request of the branch—rather, the sap is "pumped" into the branch from the vine. In like manner, it is Christ's life pouring into us that enables us to live the Christian life and to bear the hallmarks of character that we call the fruit of the Spirit. This fruit is described as being a wonderful blended mix of love, joy, peace, patience, kindness, goodness, faithfulness, gentleness, and self-control (see Galations 5:22–23).

Can you work yourself up into being an automatically loving person in every situation, to all people, consistently over time? I doubt it. Can you try and try and try to be a joyful person to the point where you suddenly become joyful always, no matter what is happening? No. It is only as we allow the Holy Spirit to do His work in us—opening ourselves continually to His power and presence—that our very nature is transformed until we develop a character and a quality of personality that truly is loving, joyful, peaceful, patient, kind, good, faithful, gentle, and under control in all situations, with all people, at all times.

The Holy Spirit is the One who authorizes, empowers, enables, and enacts a *holy* life in us—a life that is of the same substance and quality as His life.

LEARNING TO ABIDE IN HIM

The key challenge for us is to know how to abide in the Lord—as Jesus said, "He who abides in Me, and I in him, bears much fruit." Our challenge is not to bear fruit, but to abide. How do we do it?

The apostle Paul uses a different illustration to tell us how we get into an abiding position with the Lord. In Ephesians 6 he likens our abiding state to being fully clothed in the armor of God. We are challenged to put on the whole armor of God that includes:

- *Putting on the helmet of salvation.* We must recognize continually that the Lord desires to guide our thinking so that we are always acutely aware that we have been saved and that this earth is not our home. We must ask the Lord daily to help us to be aware of others He brings our way who do not know the saving power of Christ Jesus.

- *Putting on the breastplate of righteousness.* We are to recognize continually that it is the Lord who guards our emotions. We must ask the Lord daily to help us to express Him to others, not merely to react to what others say and do, but to respond to others by seeing the deep needs of their hearts and seeking to meet those needs as Christ would meet them.

- *Having our feet shod with the preparation of the gospel of peace.* We must recognize continually that the Lord desires to lead and guide our steps daily into the right paths where we can have the greatest influence and impact for the gospel. We must ask the Lord daily to help us be sensitive to where He might lead us so we can bring genuine wholeness to people.

- *Girding our loins with truth.* We are to recognize continually that it is the Lord who guards our ability to create and reproduce. We must ask the Lord daily to protect us as we create work of all types, projects of many sorts, and ministry outreaches of great diversity that will influence others. We must ask the Lord to help us produce only those things that present His truth.

- *Taking the shield of faith.* We are to recognize continually that the Lord desires to protect us from evil, and that He *will* give us the strength, wisdom, and courage we need if we will respond to life with *faith* in Christ Jesus. We must ask the Lord daily to protect us from evil.

- *Picking up the sword of the Spirit, which is the word of God.* We are to recognize that there is great power in both the written and spoken word of God—what we read from God's Word can have a life-changing effect in our lives, and what we say to others from God's Word can have a

powerful impact in defeating the devil and bringing others to salvation. We must ask the Lord daily
to sharpen our understanding of His Word and
to sharpen our ability to communicate His Word
to others.

- *Praying always with all prayer and supplication
  in the Spirit.* We must pray with perseverance as
  we petition the Lord for other believers around
  us. We are to recognize that our entire life is to
  be lived in an attitude and atmosphere of
  prayer, of constant communication and connec-
  tion with God so that we remain in a position
  to think God's thoughts of infinite wisdom and
  feel God's emotions of infinite compassion and
  love. We must ask the Lord daily to direct our
  prayers.

When you awaken tomorrow morning, I recom-
mend that you begin your day, even before you get out
of bed, by saying to the Lord:

I want to thank You, Lord, for this day. I am absolutely dependent upon You to enable me today to live the life You want me to live and to do the work You've called me to do. I choose to abide in You today. I ask You to make salvation the foremost thought in my mind, Your righteousness the foremost impulse of my heart, Your truth the foremost motivation and desire behind all I do, Your peace and wholeness the goal of all I want to accomplish. I ask You to help me walk in faith against all forms of evil. I ask You to quicken Your Word in my mind and in my mouth so that all I think and say will be in complete alignment with Your Word. I choose right now to rely upon Your Holy Spirit to give me the direction and guidance I need every minute of this day. I trust You to do this and I believe You are going to do this.

And then get up and begin to live out your day with an attitude of complete dependence upon the Lord. Listen for the Holy Spirit to speak to you deep within your being—to prompt you toward certain people and situations, to caution you against certain decisions and behaviors. Choose to be aware of His presence with you and His directives to you.

A Prayer for Intimacy with God

Many days, I find myself praying almost constantly in my mind, *God, draw me to Yourself, draw me to Yourself, draw me to Yourself.* I know that intimacy with the Lord is the place of abiding without wavering on my part and without any obstacle to the flow of the Spirit into my life. When we reach that place of deep intimacy with the Lord, we experience a joy and a peace and an overflowing sense of love that cannot be equaled. The joy we know overrides any difficulty, hardship, trial, tribulation, or lack we may have in our lives. His peace and His love fill up every lonely, frustrated, or empty crevice in our being. He deals with us in a way that is infinitely kind and good and faithful and generous and merciful, so that our automatic response to ourselves and to others is one of kindness, goodness, faithfulness, generosity, and mercy.

Yes, God, draw me to Yourself. May He draw all of us to Himself so that we move into deeper and deeper intimacy with Him every day of our lives.

I believe that when you choose to live this way—

with dependence upon the Lord, acute awareness of the Lord at work in your life, and a desire for greater intimacy with the Lord—you are going to recognize when you get to the end of the day that the Holy Spirit was at work in you to help you live a holy life.

Why don't all believers do this? Because most people want to remain in control of their own lives. They want to be "in charge" so they will feel more powerful or more adequate. Most of the success books and seminars out on the market advocate that people have self-confidence, become more self-motivated, and increase in self-importance. Friend, the Holy Spirit calls us to have confidence in God, to be motivated by His Spirit, and to place the highest importance on doing what God says to do. I want to be a person who is God confident, God directed, and God serving. That is true success. That is the way we get to the best that life has to offer.

To be entirely reliant upon the Holy Spirit is to be led into a holy life by the Spirit.

6

Recognizing *the* Ongoing Work *of the* Holy Spirit *in* Our Lives

Throughout the Bible, we find two great terms that are associated with the way the Holy Spirit works in each of our lives: power and authority.

- *Power.* There are many references that tell us that the Holy Spirit imparts to us the divine energy of God to enable us physically, emotionally, mentally, and spiritually to do what God calls us to do. This power is not only a burst of power to accomplish a given task, but a sustaining power that gives us the ability to persevere and to overcome. The power of God at work in us over time brings us to a place of great inner strength that others may perceive as confidence or boldness.

- *Authority.* The Holy Spirit is the highest authority in any situation in life. The Holy Spirit never loses authority—His authority is unchanging and never subject to being diminished. The Holy Spirit always seeks to enact obedience to the commandments of God, which are also absolute and unchanging. Those who are filled with the Holy Spirit have a bearing of authority about them—they often bear the marks of spiritual leadership, which may or may not be the same as organizational leadership.

These two words are very important for us to keep in mind as we take a look at the various works that the Holy Spirit seeks to do in every person's life. These words convey a sense that the Holy Spirit is relentless, positive, insistent, and commanding in the way He deals with us. There is nothing passive about the Holy Spirit's ongoing work in our lives. The Spirit functions in a proactive, intentional, urging, demanding, compelling way.

SEVEN WORKS OF THE
HOLY SPIRIT IN OUR LIVES

Here are seven works that the Holy Spirit does in the life of the believer *constantly:*

1. *The Holy Spirit convicts us of sin.* This is the first and foremost work of the Holy Spirit. None of us came to Christ apart from the Holy Spirit convicting us of sin. Having an awareness of sin led each of us to the recognition of our state as sinners, which in turn led to our confessing our sins to receive God's forgiveness.

After we become believers, the Holy Spirit continues to convict us of our sins so that we might confess our sins quickly to God, repent of our sinful ways, and seek to follow the Lord more closely in keeping His commandments.

2. *The Holy Spirit regenerates us.* He saves us. He cleanses us. He indwells us. He seals us forever as a child of God. Paul wrote to the Romans that the Holy Spirit was God's "earnest"—God's downpayment—money in our lives as an indicator to the enemy that we belong to God forever. After we

become believers, the Holy Spirit continues to cleanse us as we confess our sins. He continues to "wash us" so that we are free from the dust of the world's influences and temptations.

3. *The Holy Spirit teaches us and guides us.* He reminds us of things we have been taught about God and have experienced personally in our walk with the Lord. He reminds us of God's Word. He gives us words to speak when we face times of persecution or when we are asked to speak about Jesus. He leads us into all truth—He gives us insight into the meaning of the Scriptures and how to apply them (see John 16:13).

4. *The Holy Spirit comforts us.* His abiding presence helps us to withstand the criticism and persecution of others who do not know the Lord. His abiding presence helps us to deal with grief, loneliness, and anxiety. He comforts us most of all by continually seeking to make us whole—spiritually, mentally, emotionally, and physically.

5. *The Holy Spirit gives us spiritual gifts.* These gifts are of two types. The Holy Spirit gives us ministry

gifts which are uniquely ours to use in service to others. They are imparted to us in keeping with our personalities, natural traits, and God's purpose for our lives. These ministry gifts do not vary from situation to situation (see Romans 12:6–8). Every believer has one or more spiritual gifts that he is to develop and use to win souls to Christ and build up the body of Christ.

There are also supernatural gifts that the Holy Spirit imparts to a believer so that the Holy Spirit can accomplish His purposes in a specific situation or circumstance. These gifts are listed in 1 Corinthians 12:7–10. These gifts are often called manifestations of the Spirit. They are not gifts that are given *to* a believer on a permanent basis, but rather, they are gifts that flow *through* a believer on a temporary basis to meet a specific need in the body of Christ. These gifts function to build up the entire body of Christ.

Our ministry gifts and the supernatural gifts of the Spirit are used to build up the body of Christ. They are distributed according to the will of the Holy Spirit in order to bring the body of Christ as a whole into full maturity of faith.

6. *The Holy Spirit imparts His nature to us.* As we discussed earlier, the Holy Spirit bears His fruit in our lives. The more we abide in Him, the greater the fruit. He reproduces His character likeness in us so that we become human embodiments of His love, joy, peace, patience, kindness, goodness, faithfulness, gentleness, and self-control (see Galations 5:22–23).

Our embodiment of the Holy Spirit's nature is our greatest witness. Our expressions and words of love, joy, and peace are what draw others to us so they *want* to hear the gospel. Our expressions of patience, kindness, goodness, faithfulness, gentleness, and self-control say to the unbeliever, *This person has something you don't have. Find out what it is.* It is as we live in the Spirit—reflecting the nature of the Holy Spirit to others—that the Holy Spirit uses our witness to convict the unbelievers of sin.

7. *The Holy Spirit refines and transforms us so that we become more like Christ Jesus.* The six works of the

Holy Spirit refine and transform us from the inside out so that we grow and mature spiritually until we reflect the fullness of Christ Jesus. As the apostle Paul wrote to the Romans, God is continually in the process of conforming us into the image of His Son (see Romans 8:28–30).

All that the Holy Spirit does in us and through us is for our eternal benefit and ultimately, for us to bring glory to God. How wonderful, awesome, and blessed it is to have the Holy Spirit at work in your life!

Many people today seem reluctant to *want* the Holy Spirit at work in their lives. Friend, we should be seeking nothing else.

What a wonderful blessing it is to have the Holy Spirit reveal to us our sins so we might confess them, repent of them, and become free of them! What a wonderful blessing to have the Holy Spirit cleanse us of our sin so we can live free of guilt and shame!

What a wonderful blessing to feel the comforting presence of God with us in our times of need! What a wonderful blessing to have the Holy Spirit reveal to us the meaning of God's Word and to show us how to live a successful life!

What a wonderful blessing to be used by the Holy Spirit to build up the body of Christ! What a wonderful blessing to live a life in the Holy Spirit that draws others to Christ!

What a wonderful blessing to know with assurance that God is at work in our lives *always* for our benefit and His glory!

I do not see how any believer who is abiding in the Lord and who is not only open to having the Holy Spirit work in his life but is actively *seeking and desiring* the Holy Spirit to work in his life—can ever be down in the dumps. The Holy Spirit is never the cause of depression, stress, anxiety, or confusion. He is always the Solution to those conditions.

THE HOLY SPIRIT NEVER GIVES UP ON US

The Holy Spirit continues to do these seven works in our lives with power and authority. The Holy Spirit never gives up on us. He continues to convict, regenerate, comfort, teach, and guide us—with an insistent, compelling urgency. He continues to impart His gifts and to pour His life into us so that we are effective in all that we do for the Lord.

What can stop this work of the Holy Spirit in our lives? Only one thing—our refusal to allow Him to work in us. Once we are born again spiritually, we cannot *remove* the Holy Spirit from our lives, but we can willfully choose not to respond to Him as He seeks to lead and guide us daily.

Our refusal may be rooted in willful rebellion. Our refusal may also be much more subtle—it may be rooted in our doing things our way and living by our own strength. If we do not invite the Holy Spirit to work in us and through us, we do not experience the fullness of His presence or power.

The good news, however, is this: if we say yes to the Holy Spirit, He always says yes to us. He works in us to the extent we allow His power to infuse us and His authority to be established over us. As He works in us, we truly become His "workmanship, created in Christ

Jesus for good works, which God prepared beforehand that we should walk in them" (Eph. 2:10).

Won't you invite the Holy Spirit to work in you today?

7

Marks
of a
Spirit-Led
Believer

H ow can you tell if you are truly filled with the Spirit? How can you tell if you are being led by the Spirit? The Bible tells us that there are three great hallmarks of the Spirit-filled, Spirit-led believer.

- *First, the person who is filled with the Holy Spirit is going to be a person of generous, joyful, and overflowing praise and thanksgiving to God.* The Spirit-filled, Spirit-led person is going to radiate exuberance for the things of God. The apostle Paul told the church in Ephesus that those who were filled with the Spirit would find themselves "speaking to one another in psalms and hymns and spiritual songs, singing and making melody in your heart to the Lord, giving thanks always for all things to God the Father in the name of our Lord Jesus Christ" (Eph. 5:19–20). The Spirit-filled person cannot help but be overflowing with praise and joy.

- *Second, the person who is filled with the Holy Spirit is going to be willing to submit to one another in the fear of God* (see Ephesians 5:21). The Spirit-filled person is going to be so filled with love for God and others, and so willing to trust God to work in his own life and in the lives of others, that he will be willing to submit to others rather than demand his own way. He will not only lay down his pride before God, but also before others. Does this mean that the Spirit-filled believer becomes a doormat or a weakling in the face of evil and persecution? The opposite is true. In submitting to other believers, the Spirit-filled person receives the full benefit of all the gifts that the Lord desires to pour out on His church. The Spirit-filled person is nourished and cherished by the Lord. He is in the exact position required to receive the full protection and provision of the Lord.

The more a person submits his life to the Lord and to the working of the Lord through other Spirit-filled believers, the more that person is going to grow in faith and the stronger he is going to become. Submitting is not a sign of weakness. Rather, it is a key to becoming *strong*.

- *Third, the person who is filled with the Holy Spirit is going to have a great desire to win souls and to build up other believers.* The person who is filled with the Spirit is going to be an active, vocal, eager witness for Christ wherever the Spirit leads him to go! He is going to desire to see souls saved and lives changed. He is going to do whatever he can do to help the body of Christ become strong and flourish and prosper and be blessed spiritually, emotionally, and materially. He is going to have a deep desire to see the gospel preached to every person in every nation.

Ask yourself today . . . *Do I have great joy in my life? Am I eager to get up every morning to see what God has in store for me? Am I quick to voice my praise to God and to thank Him for all that He has done, is doing, and promises to do for me? Do I live in eager expectation of all that God is going to do?*

Am I willing to submit myself to others or do I cling to what I want, when I want it, and how I want it? Am I willing to trust God to work through others to accomplish His perfecting work in me? Am I willing to submit my will to His will?

Am I doing all that I can to see others come to Christ? Am I willing to speak the name of Jesus and to tell others what Jesus has done on their behalf? Am I using my spiritual gifts? Do I have a deep desire to see the body of Christ become mature and effective?

If your answer is no to any of these questions, do not question whether you have been filled with the Spirit. Rather, ask the Spirit to do more of His work in you so that your answer might become yes to these challenges!

Ask the Holy Spirit to reveal to you those sins in

your life that need to be confessed. Ask the Holy Spirit to cleanse you of your sins and give you His strength to turn from them. Ask the Holy Spirit to teach you and guide you into the ways you should go. Ask the Holy Spirit to show you how to train your own mind and thought patterns so they line up with God's Word.

Invite the Holy Spirit to do His work in you and to give you His joy, His heart, His mind, His goals, and His motivation.

8

How Do We Remain Full of the Holy Spirit?

Many people have made receiving the Holy Spirit a difficult task. Others make walking in the Spirit a difficult challenge. There is nothing complicated about either receiving or living in the presence and power of the Holy Spirit.

I grew up believing that I had to get down on my knees and pray and beg and plead and cry and hope that the Holy Spirit would come fill up my life. And if He did, my expectation was that I would have to work hard at holding on to His presence in my life. I asked myself many times, *What is going to happen to me if the Spirit fills my life? What will He make me do? How will I be able to keep Him in my life? What kind of spiritual gift will He give me and how will I know what to do with it?*

Then I came to the realization that pleading, crying, and hoping was not the way to receive the Holy Spirit.

There is only one requirement for receiving the Holy Spirit into your life and that is *believing*.

• *To believe, you must first recognize that you have a need for the forgiving power of Jesus Christ.* You must place your trust in Jesus as your Savior and accept with your whole heart that what He did at the cross of Calvary was for *your* eternal salvation. You must *believe* in Jesus as your Savior.

• *Second, you must believe that God's Word is true when it says that those who believe in Christ Jesus are indwelled by the Holy Spirit at the moment of their believing.* It is the Holy Spirit who gives us our spiritual birth in Christ Jesus. He then seals that birth forever by entering our spirit and dwelling in our innermost being so that we are *in Christ* and *Christ is in us.* We must *believe* that the Holy Spirit is resident in us.

• *Third, you must believe that God's Word is true when it says that the Holy Spirit works in you as*

your Comforter, Counselor, and Truth-Teacher.
We must believe that the gifts of the Holy Spirit
have been imparted to us and that our personal
ministry gifts have been given to us to develop
and use. We must believe that the Holy Spirit is
working in us to refine and transform us into
the people God created us to be. We each must
believe that the Holy Spirit is at work in our
lives.

All of our believing is established, of course, on the
foundation of God's Word and God's promises. Our
believing about what God has done, is doing on our
behalf, and will do for us throughout eternity is based
upon what God says. We *believe,* ultimately, that God's
Word is true and unchanging and that it applies personally and directly to us. We must come to the place
where we say:

What the Bible says about Jesus being the Savior and
dying on the cross for the remission of sins is true . . . and
it is true for me.

What the Bible says about the Holy Spirit being

given to those who believe is true . . . and it is true for me.

What the Bible says about the Holy Spirit's ongoing work in a believer's life is true . . . and it is true for me.

THREE ATTRIBUTES OF BELIEVING

Believing has three great attributes:

- *First, believing is simple.* That does not mean it is always easy. Believing requires that we put our trust in God and stop relying on our own looks, skills, abilities, talents, family heritage, social status, possessions, or intelligence. Believing requires that we lay down our own pride and lay down our reliance upon our human adequacy.

- *Second, believing involves our desire.* It is saying, "I desire what God wants more than I desire what I want." It is saying, "I desire to obey God more than I desire to run my own life according to my own standards and laws."

- *Third, believing involves our will.* It is an act of the will to confess sin and repent of sin. It is an act of the will to yield ourselves to the Holy Spirit and say to the Lord, "Not my will, but Thy will be done." It is an act of the will to say, "I will use my spiritual gifts—I will open my mouth and say what God wants me to say, I will yield my agenda and schedule and go where God wants me to go, and I will relinquish rights to my own goals and do what God wants me to do."

It is also an act of the will to say, "I will remove any hindrance in my life that keeps me from following the Holy Spirit's directives." It is up to us to remove the sin that keeps us from following the Lord freely and fully. In writing to the Ephesians, the apostle Paul made it very clear that we are to put off or put away certain behaviors so that we can be renewed in the spirit of our minds and hearts. He wrote, "The truth is in Jesus: that you put off, concerning your former conduct, the old man which grows corrupt according to the deceitful lusts, and be renewed in the spirit of your mind, and that you put on the new man which was created according to God, in true righteousness and holiness" (Eph. 4:21–24). It is up to us to *act* on what the Holy Spirit directs us to do. Until we confess and "put off" the sin that He reveals to us, He cannot work further in us.

One of the most profound and important events of my life took place one Friday afternoon about four o'clock when I read these verses of the Bible as if I was reading them for the first time:

> Now this is the confidence that we have in Him, that if we ask anything according to His will, He hears us. And if we know that He hears us, whatever we ask, we know that we have the petitions that we have asked of Him. (1 John 5:14–15)

Is it God's will that you receive the Holy Spirit into your life, that you remain "full" of the Holy Spirit, and that you walk in the presence and power of the Holy Spirit every day for the rest of your life? Absolutely!

Then you can be confident that if you say to the Holy Spirit, "I want You at work in my life and I believe You *are* at work in my life," He will answer that prayer with His very own presence.

A DAILY DECISION TO BE "FILLED"

Is being "filled" with the Holy Spirit a one time event?

Receiving the Holy Spirit is a onetime event—we receive the Holy Spirit when we receive Christ as our Savior. Once we have been born again spiritually and have received the Holy Spirit into our lives, we can never be "unbirthed." We can never put ourselves into a position where the Holy Spirit is no longer with us or in us. What the Holy Spirit does to transform our nature is lasting and irreversible.

We can, however, choose not to grow in the Lord. The decision to *grow* and to *keep on growing* is a decision that we must continue to make every day of our lives. *We must choose to be filled with the Holy Spirit each and every day.*

Every day, ask the Holy Spirit to fill your life anew

with His life-giving, joy-producing, comforting, guiding, renewing presence.

Every day, ask the Holy Spirit to fill you anew with His love, His peace, His truth.

Every day, ask the Holy Spirit to fill you to overflowing with His compassion for others.

Can a person continue to be filled again and again and again and again? Absolutely. We receive the Holy Spirit once. We are *filled* with the fullness of God's power and presence in an ongoing way as we continue to ask Him to do His work in us and through us day by day by day by day. Being filled with the Holy Spirit is something we must seek every day of our lives.

How do you receive the Holy Spirit? By believing and receiving.

How do you stay filled with the Holy Spirit so that you are growing in your faith and being effective in your witness? By believing and receiving.

How do you walk in the Holy Spirit every day for the rest of the your life? By believing and receiving.

So let me ask you . . . Have you accepted Jesus as your Savior? Have you received His promised gift of the Holy Spirit? Are you walking in the Spirit? Is the Spirit actively renewing and transforming and refining your life? Are you experiencing the blessed joy that comes with living the Spirit-led life?

I pray your answer is yes to all of these questions. If not, lay down control of your life today. Confess whatever sin God brings to your mind. Ask God to forgive you and cleanse you. Thank Him for filling you with His Spirit. Invite Him to take full authority over your life and to do in you and through you whatever He desires. Begin to thank and praise Him for His presence with you always.

Friend, if you will do these things, the joy of the Spirit-led life is going to be yours!

ABOUT THE AUTHOR

DR. CHARLES F. STANLEY is pastor of the 15,000-member First Baptist Church in Atlanta, Georgia, and is president and CEO of In Touch® Ministries. He has twice been elected president of the Southern Baptist Convention and is well known internationally through his IN TOUCH radio and television ministry. His many *New York Times* bestselling books include *Walking Wisely, When Tragedy Strikes, Charles Stanley's Handbook for Christian Living, Finding Peace, When the Enemy Strikes, A Touch of His Power, Our Unmet Needs, Enter His Gates,* and *The Source of My Strength.*

ALSO FROM
DR. CHARLES F. STANLEY

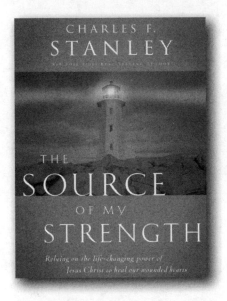

ISBN 0-7852-8273-4
AVAILABLE AT BOOKSTORES EVERYWHERE

Pastor and bestselling author Dr. Charles F. Stanley
offers hope to the broken-hearted and guides readers
toward strength in Christ.

NELSON BOOKS
A Division of Thomas Nelson Publishers
Since 1798

www.thomasnelson.com

ALSO FROM
DR. CHARLES F. STANLEY

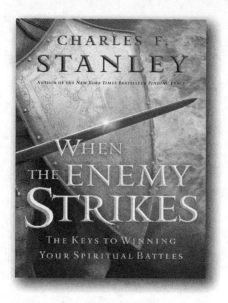

ISBN 0-7852-6610-0
AVAILABLE AT BOOKSTORES EVERYWHERE

Dr. Charles F. Stanley shows readers how to have
victory over the Enemy by drawing from the same
divine power that created the heavens and earth.

NELSON BOOKS
A Division of Thomas Nelson Publishers
Since 1798

www.thomasnelson.com